SOMETHING LIKE A RIVER

SOMETHING LIKE A RIVER

Roberta Feins

MoonPath Press

Poetry
ISBN 978-1-936657-11-7

Cover photo: "Sunrise at Sea, Cape Disappointment"
mixed media assemblage (painted and cut driftwood),
27" x 13" x 1", 2010
by David Francis

Author photo: Bill Ross

Design by Tonya Namura
using Optima

MoonPath Press is dedicated to publishing the
best poets of the U.S. Northwest Pacific states

MoonPath Press
PO Box 1808
Kingston, WA 98346

MoonPathPress@yahoo.com

http://MoonPathPress.com

To Bill

Acknowledgements

I acknowledge with thanks, the following journals where these poems originally appeared, sometimes in different name and form:

Turn of River: *BlueLine* Vol 32 2011

Easter Feast: *OVS (Organs of Vision and Speech)*, Spring 2012

Nature of America Series: *Windfall* Spring 2011

I-97 North: *Avocet*, Vol XII, No. 2 Winter 2009

Kenai Fiords, Alaska: *The Naugatuck River Review*, Issue 4 Summer 2010

After Li-Po's Song on Bringing in the Wine: *Tattoo Highway Issue* 20, 2010

Though I live West, My Heart is East: *BlueLine* Vol 32 2011

Kittitas County 2: Town Park: *Camas*, 2012

Kittitas County 5: Thorp Mill: *Camas*, 2012

Tashlich Service: *Poetica* 2009 Holiday Edition

Etude: *Long Story Short*, September 2009

Seasonal Memoir: *Wilderness House Literary Review* Spring 2007

Razor Clam Season at Ocean Shores: *Flyway: Journal of Writing and Environment* Vol 12, # 3, 2010

Thank you to my poetry critique buddies: Susan Sailer, Janet Barry and John Krumberger, the Village Idioms, Lindsey Royce, Steve Riel, Laura Snyder, Deborah Woodard, the faculty and students at New England College.

Gratitude to Lana Hechtmann Ayers for providing a venue for publication.

Contents

Moon Ode: Fall   3
Turn of River   4
Easter Feast   5
Nature of America Series   6
We Were Not Citizens of That Town,   7
I-97 North   9
Ayalik Bay, Alaska   11
After Li-Po's *Song on Bringing in the Wine*   13
July, Paradise, Mt. Rainier   14
Though I live West, My Heart is East   16
Something Like A River   17
Polar Route   18
Tiffany Lake
    i.   20
    ii.   21
Kittitas County
    1: Ranch Bed and Breakfast   22
    2: Town Park   23
    3: Upper Yakima Valley   24
    4: Roslyn   25
    5: Thorp Mill   26
Tashlich Service   28
Seasonal Memoir
    i.   30
    ii.   31
    iii.   32
    iv.   33
Cold Climate   34
Razor Clam Season at Ocean Shores   35

About the Author   36

SOMETHING LIKE A RIVER

Moon Ode: Fall

September bronze hills stood still
while birds hurried by on obliging winds.
The soul rang clear in the night, boot heels
on the sidewalks of an Old West town.

Cedars faced me openly,
but meadow grasses only sighed and lay down.
The reaper plowed a swath, baled
their last words, wrapped them with plastic skin.

Thursday night, I opened all the windows,
raised my eyes to the luminous moon.
Suddenly, earth and I changed places;
I lay down to better bear the weight.

Turn of River

An open January, the Connecticut still rolls
gelid amid glinting floes. I was born
where rivers flow wide, straight to the sea

great port at the confluence: never
learned the winding ox-bow, curve
of Indian Corn Mill Road, hand-cut tattered

house boards. Stubbled rocks, split-grain,
groin and tilt in weighty dance.
The map's filled with crossroads, cemeteries,

relatives' addresses. Towns are no closer
but haven't grown apart either. Friendly
restaurants beckon; spiny roof vanes

prick like church spires. Whatever I am
I took from this landscape. Red beacons flash
from smokestacks of abandoned mills;

fabled towns are buckled concrete, slipping
heaps of garbage tunneled by colonial rats.
Along the verge, red sumac candelabra

burn against bare trees. When did I become
the pound of flesh the East tried to reclaim?
Driving south, snow thins. Near Concord,

each blade and rush glitters within brittle
filaments of ice. The roofs of used cars
gleam in the same unseasonable light.

Easter Feast

Your hands have rubbed the lamb
with rosemary, garlic, olive oil, salt.
While the leg roasts at 500 degrees,
we make love, juicy smell of flesh
drifts the house. Garlic, licked from your fingers,
makes my mouth water with desire.
Boneless muscle seared in the heat
of intense pleasure, almost pain.

Oh, the sacrament of you in body
age lifts, years roll away;
we lie again in the dry canyon, yellow-
headed blackbirds chirring in creek willows.
Shy then, we were modest; only apples,
cheese for our belated picnic. Now,
meat roasts in our childless oven.
We are both sizzling carrion and bleating newborns.

Nature of America Series

At the Post Office, I buy a pane
of stamps: painting of an Eastern forest.
As I pull off each stamp, the forest
disappears: black bear,

Northern Oak, weasel. Later,
on a walk by Seattle Viewlands school,
I touch soft fir-tips, dodge
nettles springing beside the sandy path.

Black-vested towhees forage
in a gravel pile; the un-mowed meadow,
a snarl of invaders—blackberries, scotch
broom, starlings—also a haven

for quail, coyote, hummingbirds.
Warblers arrive, trill atop
the shed where last year they nested,
safe from cats, next to tomato cages,

mower, plastic fence, sprinkler.
The bees that work a patch of thyme
dance the same measure as if
they lived in the first Garden.

I want to study the etched and hachured lines,
see more clearly than in the finest micrograph
whether it is all falling together
or peeling apart.

We Were Not Citizens of That Town,

famous for its raceway,
as spelled in red neon letters, lighting
one after the other across the dusky horizon.

We never went to the track—of course
I was too young to go—but I mean my parents

never gambled, or even just leaned
at the rail, watching those poor creatures
play out their nature in harness.

We lived at the parkway's other end,
where there were trees, and broken glass

didn't glint from the gutters, read
only the New York Times, shopped
at delis and bakeries under the rumble

of the Jerome/Woodlawn elevated line.
I often caught the bus to the Bronx,
rode past the banked oval, took the subway

to the Metropolitan Museum, to admire
bronze votive horses, Greek kraters,
an archaic kouros stilled in white marble.

Coming home after dark, on a late,
almost-empty bus, there was one moment

where the swoop of wall and ramp
let me see beyond the wall—the ring
softened by flood lights, thousands in the stands,

and, like a precious painted kylix, black
shadows of horses pulling shadows of sulkies.

I-97 North

We are driving home from visiting a country of long
        round hills
where it rarely rains, and water from snow-melt rivers
imparts its own erratic beat to grasses' bloom. It's May;
cattle have been loosed to graze where, a few weeks ago,
Sandhill Cranes clattered and leapt in their awkward
        love-frenzy.

At night above our tent, Great-Horned Owls chanted to
        the moon;
Canyon Wrens woke us with their slowing, falling trill.
As sun cleared the rimrock, rime melted from grass;
a chunky black and white merganser winged upstream,
low over the creek's braided riot. Now, the bridge

over the Columbia forms the perfect arc of the word dry.
We stop at dusk in a park, unnaturally green, hissing with
        sprinklers.
Gulls wait anxiously for their next meal, preparing
for combat even before we leave our picnic.
We follow red eyes of cars ahead, up the mounded breasts

of Manastash Ridge, winding through the Firing Range,
where, tomorrow at dawn, sage grouse will strut and boom
on the fresh wheatgrass of their leks. White firefly
headlights dart past the other way, back down to the
        desert.

Unable to resist, we sneak a last look back. But, behind us
the full song has slipped, hushed. In the world we
        are rejoining,
rain is the sky's vocation, monotonous hours of drip
        and spatter.
We hear drops ping on the roof, the wipers' steady huff.

Ayalik Bay, Alaska

Tiny kinglets sing: brilliant, incessant
from each thicket of scrub willow. Here,
all that belongs to earth and water loves song.

Melt-water drips
in countless variant waterfalls.
Retreating snow has left this beach
just wide enough for us to camp.

Each day I paddle, dipping my blade
into this cold soup of sea
in front of glacier, land
crouched at every inlet's end,

paws of snow reaching to water.
Blue-streaked columns busy themselves
shattering: constant crack and thunder.

Hurried by tide and current,
I use my strength to turn and guide
as best I can. All enigmas seem absurd;
I'm in a trance —

a flexible bow pushing, pulling
long wings through watery sky
whose clouds are solid bits of ice,
prisms, snowballs, sculptures, slabs.

Breeze in my face carries
the stench and grunt of fat seals
basking on nearby rocks.

Tonight, we camp in pine scrub,
in front of a vast meadow.
Beached bergs melt like candles,
tunneled by rills of clear water.

I trace a path through grass and mud,
Waddling in my dry suit pelt,
looking for a place to crouch.
On the way back, fresh prints –

lobed mudflowers of bear paws –
cross my track. Night
comes down, late, to bathe in the sea.
I hear the high truth of cobbles
tumbled by tide.

After Li-Po's *Song on Bringing in the Wine*

See how the Columbia River
pours from the Canadian Cascades,
races wildly to the Pacific, never returns.
Fix your hair in the hall mirror, dear.

Just yesterday, we were natural brunettes;
this evening's color pours from a bottle.
Never mind. An empty smile makes the moon cry.

Forget our crass bosses, investment failures,
losing Scratch Ticket. Let's just wave
our plastic at the clerk, grab
the Pale Ale, nachos, Ballard Bitter.

Remember the time we dragged Jeff
down Mission Street by his coat collar?
We'll be telling that story long after

the ping of acoustic sensors finds
no salmon left to count. Turn up the music,
let's dance to that song Ralph played
on his tinny tape deck at Rocky Reach.

July, Paradise, Mt. Rainier

A palette of alpine meadow licks my dazzled eyes.
    Mesmerized.
Dark firs scatter brilliant green across a bowl
    of snowy hills.

Streams and rills.
Waterfalls.

High glaciers' walls of turquoise shaped this ground,
roar and flood grind this soil, feed the brood of bloom:

gush,
then trickle of spill.

Shooting Stars flourish in muddy runnels,
    soap-bubbles
of Partridge Foot carpet glades marked
    by fluted funnels
of deep blue Gentian. Plumes of Beargrass:

wax-nubbed rockets,
radiate tails
of immaculate fox.

Bracted Lousewort's hollow petals shape
to the sickle tongues of hummingbirds.
Pasqueflower's past flower,
wearing a wig of swollen cotton-floss.

In rocky niche
the smallest, fragile,

beaded drop
drips

to feed notch-edged leaves of Saxifrage,
    cushions of moss.
Gray leaves of Pussy Toes furl tight
    against the umbel sun, itself

a flooded flower,
carmine
incarnate.

Though I live West, My Heart is East

At Watervleit Shaker Village, I stroll
a flea market in its 1848 meeting house.
Visiting Albany, where I lived
in my seventeenth to twenty-third years,

I drive streets which still grid my dreams—
Price Chopper grocery store, alley of old maples—
squeeze nostalgia from an exit ramp
where I stalled, learning to drive stick.

At the granite gray State Capitol,
my heart strobed to the flash and clamor of politics.
Born on this coast, where the sun rises over ocean,
small prey for my taloned superiors, all the words

they used to name me choked tight, spelled failure.
North winds swirled down the wintry Hudson,
moaning through grates on the Rensselaer Bridge.
I moved West, where the sun sets over ocean,

summers are cool, woods green even in winter.
Any time I come back, I smell
traps of tar bubbling in hot streets. Tonight,
a table is prepared in the presence of my relatives,

loaded with food for which I hunger:
pickles, whitefish. In summer, roadsides riot
with sparklers of flowering milkweed,
wild blue lupine, plumes of poison sumac.

Something Like A River

In the photo of my third-grade class
I see our futures revealed as forms of water.

Rich, pedaling a carton of egg foo-yung
to an air-conditioned apartment in midtown
        Manhattan,
is a drop of sweat on a muggy afternoon.

Jerry evaporates from a beer glass,
only a foamy trace left on the rim.

Robin's tears flood the TV room.
She waits for the garage door's rumble,
prelude to her lover's fists.

The spot of blood at the needle's tip
is Lowell, drowning in the milk fed to his son.

My lecture on The Next Generation:
three drops spilled from the garden hose I left
sprawled by the parched lawn.

Ellen's children know her as pure cold,
a cracked icicle lodged in their hearts.

Billy still searches for thirst. He has become
a Byzantine aqueduct;
storks nest on his grooved ledges.

Mrs. Hurley was the bead in a carpenter's plane
our balance & tilt. Together, we were once
something like a river, something like a cloud.

Polar Route

Greenland is a grenadier's hat, pleated
black ribbon basted
          along the hillsides.

Glaciers spread out gracious crinoline.
Creased white shirts popping open
to the sea
          at the breastline.

Braided rivers are smoother,
without ridges or rocks, just
frozen waves beaten
          by the gale

against the shore. Windrows plow
the bleached sea like shoals of dolphins.
The hills are layered
          petit fours.

There is still so much snow, even
in summer sun. We make a great shadow.
Once, only a shaman
          would have had this view

in trance, flying to the spirit world
to the beat of a drum, to diagnose
          an illness, an emptiness.

Our flight destroys the landscape we admire.
Great basalt pyramids of mountains
lie bared to sky. This brood and melt
                    our harvest.

In the screen of the seat ahead
a woman fixes her lipstick
in the reflection
                    of the Island.

Tiffany Lake

Reading Tranströmer in Eastern Washington

i.

The North Wind uses branches to scribble on the sky.
Though his work is admired,
he visits too rarely to be god of this valley.

His spouse, dry Earth,
sucks water from shrinking creeks, waits
for his return through long summer months.

Her anger lights votive clusters
of chokecherry, sets yellow leaves
of columbine aflame. She whirls dust
to lay a pall over beauty,
muting birds with the screech of chain-saws.

ii.

Morning after the storm:
ground blooded with leaves, bare trees
leafed with light, the way a death
lets you see your life clearly.

How could that be, when your animal soul
curls grief like a tail over your eyes?

Kittitas County

1: Ranch Bed and Breakfast

The Native American meaning of *Kittitas*
is unclear; I prefer the translation:
a broad resting place by water
like this ranch, growing hay, sheep,
pasturing draft horses and paying guests,
at a bend in the Yakima River.

Our bedroom is next to the concrete tack room.
Cowboy boots, sizes small to large,
line one shelf. Black and silver harness
hangs on pegs below. There's a lot of capital

sunk into horseflesh and machines
both old and new: tractors, a harvester,
wagons, a grader. *We'll have to break up*
the land and the gear into lots
to be able to sell it in this economy,

Heather says. She can't ride anymore,
needs to be closer to city doctors.
A young chestnut mare returns from pasture,
stepping delicately through the paddock
to her stall.

She still misses her mother.
We hear her kicking through the night.
In spite of strong winds from the north,
in spite of all the beauty that remains
I can't forgive her loss.

2: Town Park

My feet step lightly among the fallen fruit,
my hands reach down once and again
to lift and hold the warm, un-bruised sum
of season, soil, water. Ripening
is just a mechanical unfolding
of helix and molecule, enzyme and sugar.
Still, in this plum, I bring *autumn*
and *mature* to my mouth. I suck these words
like a pit beneath my tongue.

3: Upper Yakima Valley

I am bargaining with a cottonwood
to tell my whole life story. His mossy arms
reach out, a peddler offering
just the right shade of blue ribbon
to brighten the lonely farm-wife's hair.

My tale is open to multiple readings.
It took me only fifty years
to jumble the chronology, as if

I'd forgotten a nursery rhyme's first verse
as soon as I learned the second.
There was something—*hm, hm, hm*—
about power, something—*la, la, la*—
about the hidden wealth of trees.

4: Roslyn

Town cemetery's made up
of twenty-six sections, men sorted
by language, country, religion and lodge.

Slag piles and politics are dirty business.
It's hard for me to choose sides,
even one hundred and twenty-years later.

Each clapboard house has a rough shed
out back. There, the miners would wash and change.
Hollyhocks grow by the boarded windows,

weathered tram cars rot slowly
among chicory and knapweed
in a lot scattered with windfall apples.

In the Town Museum, framed clippings
reporting mine explosions jostle
silk banners of the Daughters of Pythias.

A mine manager was tied to the tracks
by striking lawless miners, and saved
at-the-last-minute by the loyal train engineer.

In 1888, the Northern Pacific Company
integrated the town by hiring
three hundred Negro strikebreakers.

We rummage through the stereopticon slides.
Each pair shows the same scene
from only two angles at once.

5: Thorp Mill

Enthusiastic weeds grow by the canal,
drink quick, cold water. A turbine shaft
rusts among them. We stand beside
an old cracked wheel belted with iron.

Our voices grind at the past, conjuring
wagons of wheat sifting into the mill
to be ground, bagged, shipped to market.

The engine of progress no longer requires
leather belts and wooden wheels,
or ice hauled by draft horses
finished with the fall's haying,
stored in sawdust to cool summer produce
flowing east by train. Years ago,

someone breached the dam, swept away
twists of wire fastening the bales.

But the past's still piled, un-threshed,
in my heart. I can't remember
horses pulling the load, I only see
faded photos pasted to weathered signs,
imagine blowing snow frozen to their lashes.

I am trying to separate weed from wildflower,
wheat from chaff. It can be done with augur hoists,
paddle bars, steam or stream. But I see only how

then and now are harnessed together,
how the dialect of the interstate
is descended from the railroad's language,
the river's precise diction.

Tashlich Service

Our tattered bellbottoms brush the dirt;
we clamber down the path to the river.
New Youth Group we hardly know each other,
flirting and sincere, eager

for experience the September day we go down
to the wasteland to worship, down
to the river to throw away our sins.
Rusted carts, sick-sweet smell of ailanthus,

pushing its freckled green knuckles
thru piles of returnables never redeemed.
Corroded rails lead in and out of yards
where trains once carried iron from barges

to factories that made amazing objects
nobody needs today: corset stays,
grappling hooks, piano rolls, dumb -
waiters, harness rings, adding tapes.

Planks of the pier a crooked keyboard;
the river calls up through the gaps.
Bottle in one arm, fishing rod crooked in the other,
a drunk stares at us a long time, wondering if

he'd pulled us from the river of his sleep.
He offers us a drink. He offers us seats
on the pilings next to his empty bucket.
Mike strums his guitar; we read

poetry written for the service, then
fling our baby sins into the water
with hardly time to hold their breath.
Like tiny gnats, they dap the surface

of the great streaming creature that could throw back
    at us
terrible things we cannot yet imagine:
ambitions of empire, running downstream
with sloops and barges of apples, gloves and shoes,
against a tide of bony rutting shad.

Seasonal Memoir

i.

we hunched our shoulders and shook fingers
straining to see each other through air
both crystalline and opaque. Like jello,
clouded with fruit juice
(which would explain the shaking).

I walked to school with my nose in a book, until
(autumn wind peppered me with leaves)
I was ready to turn the page. Maybe

that was my undoing, what ruined everything.
The way water can be drought or flood,
but doesn't depend on point of view. No,
it's flowing; try and stay. Well, you can try.

ii.

The tabby was a threat. As softly as it jumped
and landed on the windowsill, the shadow
of nineteen fifty-six woke hissing.

The guest room always stood empty
because *had been there* was where
the rebar was buried—foundation, lattice.

My sister and I—
no matter how we grew and clung,
we were still simple annuals.

We are talking time as a sleeping bear,
an inadequate supply of batteries,
a box of crochet thread so old,
it easily breaks and ravels.

Generations of mice in lollipop heaven,
fed on the dog biscuit prom-corsage.
I got home just as they were discarding the last
     wrapper,
just as the last Romeo was buttoning his jeans.

iii.

The finches have learned the lessons of a star.
Love alone - the slow deliberate twining
of grass into nest lined with thistledown
and strands of tabby hair, trip after trip

to the seed feeder stuffing red-gaped
baby frogmouths, a singer closing his beak
so his son can bubble and stutter in squeaky
practice trills—love alone

will not satisfy a thwarted sun.
He turns and chills the North with bitter,
bloodshot eye. Under his malice,
the parents take wing, wheel
one circle above the yard and fly on south.

The fledglings follow or fall.

iv.

Moon's thinking of leaving too.
Daily she suffers, pallid in the sky
low below the horizon, rounding
herself pleasantly, trying to glow,

but clearly ignored. Even at night
people prefer cathode rays
bright and arced with story. She
just can't blurt out all she feels.

Her story takes a month,
as told by nibbling mice.
Her craters smile as she wastes away,
then waxes again, criticized
for putting on weight.

Cold Climate

Listen, my heart thunks
like the steam pipes, puncturing
the hissing monologue
of demented radiators. We lie down
near its clattering ridges,

down on the Turkish red carpet.
I justify while you mention
button by button my gauzy
blouse unwinding each white bandage
till I can't help but feel.

Steam huffs towards the merging
clouds of our breathing, cool
by the time it reaches True North
of your navel. Naked windows tremble
with each gust. Our clothes are a nest;

we are the eggs. But in this Ice Age
how incubate, how open? Man
of the egg, smoothly I cup your smooth.
Coddle me. Heat me. Snowy owl cry,
teakettle's boil, my cracked shell.

Soon, I will move white through the dusk,
past the banister's stalactites, to heat soup,
toast bread, with one finger, draw a pierced heart
on the kitchen pane. For now,
wrap the rug, red around us so we can sleep.

Razor Clam Season at Ocean Shores

Last day of the year; four o'clock
twilight, low tide. Buckets and boots.
Boots and slicker. Moon,

white-orange half-shell.
The clams are spade-shaped tubes
digging deep into wet sand,

foot a thick tongue
speaking water's quick language,
precise diction of sand grains.

Dad rocks the shovel at an angle,
digs deep, pulls hard.
Six-month old Henry

with his bottle, great-Grandma
in her lawn-chair, all take turns
twisting pulling. Teflon pan,

cornmeal batter. Dad wakes
later in the dark from a dream
of hiss and suck, the clam gun

pulling up the moon. Opens
plasticized curtains—there she is
still in the sky, sieving the morning stars.

About the Author

Roberta Feins was born in New York, and has lived in North Carolina and Seattle. She has degrees in Social Science (BA) and Marine Ecology (MS), and received her MFA in poetry in 2007 from New England College where she studied with Judith Hall, Carol Frost, DA Powell and Alicia Ostriker.

Roberta's poems have been published in *Five AM*, *Antioch Review*, *The Cortland Review* and *The Gettysburg Review*, among others. Prizes include First Prize in Poetry, *Women in Judaism's* 2010 Writing Competition, and Second Place in the 2007 Society for Humanistic Anthropology Ethnographic Poetry Competition.

Roberta edits the e-zine *Switched On Gutenberg* (http://www.switched-ongutenberg.org/) and has selected poetry for *Drash: Northwest Mosaic* and the *Naugatuck River Review*.

www.ingramcontent.com/pod-product-compliance
Lightning Source LLC
Chambersburg PA
CBHW022346040426
42449CB00006B/746